"Daily Readings for Difficult Days" is written to women who are on the edge, going through trial, suffering or pain and wondering why God has allowed this to happen and how they can get through it.

Drawing from her own experiences as a Christian for over thirty years, Jennifer Carter shares stories, testimony and scripture to encourage and inspire.

Daily Readings for Difficult Days

Copyright © 2011 Jennifer Carter

Published by Hope Books Ltd (www.hopebooks.org)

All Rights Reserved. No part of this publication may be reproduced in any form or by any means, including scanning, photocopying, or otherwise without prior written permission of the copyright holder.

Disclaimer and Terms of Use: The Author and Publisher has strived to be as accurate and complete as possible in the creation of this book, notwithstanding the fact that he does not warrant or represent at any time that the contents within are accurate due to the rapidly changing nature of the Internet. While all attempts have been made to verify information provided in this publication, the Author and Publisher assumes no responsibility for errors, omissions, or contrary interpretation of the subject matter herein. Any perceived slights of specific persons, peoples, or organizations are unintentional. In practical advice books, like anything else in life, there are no guarantees of any kind made.

This book is not intended for use as a source of advice, readers are advised to seek services of competent professionals.

Scriptures taken from the Holy Bible,

New International Version®, NIV®.

Copyright © 1973, 1978, 1984 by Biblica, Inc.™

Used by permission of Zondervan.

All rights reserved worldwide.

www.zondervan.com

Scripture taken from The Message.

Copyright 1993, 1994, 1995, 1996, 2000, 2001, 2002.

Used by permission of NavPress Publishing Group.

Graphic Design & Layout: Melissa Caron - Enki Communications - Go-Enki.com

First Printing, 2011

ISBN 978-1-90856-7000

Daily Readings for Difficult Days

Daily Devotions for Christian Women going through Difficult Times

Jennifer Carter

Table of Contents

The First Day 11
The Second Day 13
The Third Day 15
The Fourth Day 17
The Fifth Day 19
The Sixth Day 21
The Seventh Day 23
The Eighth Day 27
The Ninth Day 29
The Tenth Day 31
The Eleventh Day 33
The Twelfth Day 35
The Thirteenth Day 37
The Fourteenth Day 39
The Fifteenth Day 41
The Sixteenth Day 43
The Seventeenth Day 45
The Eighteenth Day 47
The Nineteenth Day 49
The Twentieth Day 51

The Twenty First Day..53
The Twenty Second Day 55
The Twenty Third Day 57
The Twenty-Fourth Day...59
The Twenty-Fifth Day..61
The Twenty-Sixth Day 63
The Twenty-Seventh Day...65
The Twenty-Eighth Day 67
The Twenty-Ninth Day 69
The Thirtieth Day..71
The Thirty-First Day 73
A Final Word or Two...75
About the Author...77

"For God so loved the world that He gave his one and only son, that whosoever believeth in Him should not perish but have everlasting life"
John 3:16

About This Book

These writings were first compiled when I was corresponding with a young prison inmate called Brian.

Brian had become a Christian but was struggling to cope with the dark and difficult surroundings that he found himself in. I originally wrote these daily inspirations for him as a way to share my own experiences of how God can break into the darkest days of our lives.

Sadly whilst my children were still quite young, my Christian marriage broke up and ended in divorce. The process of dealing with the break up and the divorce took years to come to terms with and to come to a place for God to really heal my heart.

I hope that you will find small encouragements as you read through these pages – as I did from the way that God has, and continues to, break in on our lives.

Feel free to dip and browse through these daily readings.

Each reading is simply entitled from "The First Day" to "The Thirty-First Day", and are designed to be read in chronological order, or feel free to dip into the book if that suits your reading style.

It's funny how God catches your attention in the small things. During the darkest period of my life a friend told me that each day there would be some small thing that would point me back to God.

Despite my certainty that God was far away, certainly a million miles away from me, each day there was indeed always some small thing that reminded me of Him. Sometimes it was as seemingly insignificant as the light on a raindrop, a butterfly crossing my gaze, an unexpected smile or kindness or the colour of a leaf. No day passed where there wasn't at least one small thing to point me back to my Creator.

As I write, winter is setting in. Days are getting shorter and the whole world seems to be closing in on itself. Imagine my surprise as I innocently bustled my way from car park to local store to see the light catching the branches of a tree – nothing surprising you may say. What struck me is that, even now, before the harshest day of winter has come, the buds of next year's leaves are already furled up waiting for that first warm day of spring.

Even in our darkest times there is the promise of something better to come, if we can only believe & stand firm. As surely as the seasons come & go, so the dark times eventually pass and a brighter time arrives. Yet just as in the winter it is so hard to remember the feel of the warm sun beating down on your skin, in the dark times we need to remember that God is faithful and He promises to be with us through the darkest of days.

Today's reading:

"And surely I am with you always,
to the very end of the age."
Matthew 28:20

It was a beautiful day and the young woman was practically skipping along the road, certain that she must be elevated a good few inches above the pavement, so great was the joy that she felt. She had finally been set free – from all the great weight that had held her down all her life, her own failures, the expectations of others, pain and disappointment. All these had dropped away and she could understand the real meaning of 'freedom' for the first time in her life.

For some weeks she had been talking through issues with a young evangelist called April. Finally that day she had decided to commit her life to God and to ask Him for forgiveness of all that she had done wrong.

That young woman was me & happy as I was that day, it took me many years to fully understand that my choice that day was not just in receiving the greatest gift ever. It was also to mean that I was to give something back – myself, to become a friend of God.

The Bible tells us that we are created for relationship with God and nothing else will truly satisfy the hunger inside us. He longs for us to be His friends – to share our hearts with Him. Knowing Him IS the 'abundant life' of which the Bible speaks – it isn't a sometime thing, we don't have to wait, it is for us to begin right now.

Just as asking His forgiveness was a choice, so is our friendship with Him – the only One who is faithful and who will never fail us. What choice will you make today?

Today's reading:

"Now to Him who is able to exceedingly abundantly above all we can ask or think, according to the power that works in us."
Ephesians 3:20

If I asked you to picture the image of a young child just taking its first steps towards its loving parents – perhaps you could almost hear them encouraging the child on with arms open wide. When the child falls they are there to pick it up and encourage it to try one more time. Within a short time the child will be walking and the proud parents will be telling everyone all about it! Yet the child has tried the same thing and failed dozens and dozens of times before he or she finally succeeds.

In today's society many of us are afraid of looking like a fool. Even when we think God may have spoken to us – we wonder what will happen if we are wrong. What will people say – either to us or behind our backs?

Maybe we should instead look towards the heavens and consider, what is our Father thinking? He is that same proud parent, our Father – encouraging us forward – picking us up when we fall and so proud as we grow and develop. Yes, we may get it wrong from time – we are only human – but the smile on the Fathers face each time we choose to trust Him should encourage us to persevere.

If we do so, we will learn every nuance of His voice, from the stern Father's warning, to the quiet voice, to Him whispering "I love you my child".

Today's reading:

"The eternal God is your refuge, and underneath are the everlasting arms"
Deuteronomy 33:27

The Bible tells us that we are <u>being made</u> perfect. Sometimes we look around us at other Christians and see them as far more perfect than they are.

Once you genuinely start talking with any Christian, you're likely to find that they too feel that they are far from perfect, often acutely aware of the ways that they fail and fall short of all that they feel God has called them to.

The great thing about our Christian walk is not that we won't ever make another mistake – rather we know <u>where to turn</u> when we fall. If we go to the throne of God for forgiveness we can be sure of a hearing every time, we can be sure of Gods grace, forgiveness and loving acceptance if we come with humble and contrite hearts before Him.

Never make the mistake of turning <u>from</u> God because you've made a mistake – that's exactly when you need to turn to him. He is our patient, loving Father – far more willing to forgive us than we are to ask for forgiveness.

We're not perfect, just forgiven.

Today's reading:

"Humble yourselves before the Lord, and he will lift you up."
James 4:10

It's so easy to worry about tomorrow. Sometimes we are tempted to look weeks or months ahead to events that we are anxious about. At times like this it can be all too easy to sink into darkness and despair at the prospect of the future. We worry and become anxious – what will we say, how will we act or respond? Yet the event is 95% likely to never happen at all!

The good news is that God has given us everything that we need for TODAY. Today He will provide the strength that we need, the words to say, the comfort that we seek. The Word says "*I will ask the Father, and he will give you another Counsellor (or comforter) to be with you forever*" John 14:16

That's a promise from God to you.

A story of the great evangelist Smith Wigglesworth tells the story of him leaving his home town to go preaching where God had called him. He knew many of his friends and family would be accompanying him to the railway station, he also knew that he didn't have enough money to pay for the train ticket. As he was remonstrating with God, God spoke to him and asked him to trust Him and act as if he was going to catch the train. So he went to the station and with his friends and family excitedly around him he stood in the queue for the ticket office knowing he didn't have enough money to pay the fare. Just as he got to the counter a friend came and pressed some money into his hand. By the time he got on the train he had been given sufficient money for the entire trip. God came through as He had promised he would.

In the same way, as we trust God, He will always deliver what we need today – even though it sometimes seems to us to be at the last minute.

Today's reading:

"My grace is sufficient for you, my power is made perfect in weakness"
2 Corinthians 12:9

We began by considering how God breaks into our lives in small ways – the unexpected rainbow, a view at a turn in the road, a ray of sun on a grey day – all examples of His amazing grace. Each one of these unearned and unexpected pleasures can surprise us with joy.

Maybe that is why we all love that experience of romantic love – those first few days and weeks of being "in love". For once in our lives we are accepted for "who we are" – something satisfies that longing held deep within each of our souls.

Each one of us has experienced both grace and "ungrace". We can find ourselves crushed by a thoughtless or harsh word. And yes, it can even happen in church or with Christian friends. May God give us all opportunities to show and share His grace. Small kindnesses, words of encouragement, even a smile – can break in upon a life and make a difference.

Today's reading:

"Be kind and compassionate to one another, forgiving each other, just as in Christ God forgave you"
Ephesians 4:32

Do you sometimes feel as if the heavens are like brass? Are you asking why God isn't providing you with that miracle or moving that mountain?

Reading Mark 11:22-26 shows that answered prayer is conditional upon us forgiving others.

So how does unforgiveness affect our lives? We often think that by shutting people out and hardening our hearts to them when they hurt us that we are putting THEM in prison. The Bible reveals that if we do NOT forgive it is US who are put in prison, thus losing our own freedom.

You've probably met individuals whose lives are twisted up with anger, hate and bitterness – yet many of them have had opportunities for their lives to be different – to forgive and let go but have chosen to cling on to their feelings.

Today, make a choice. Let go of people you thought you had been keeping prisoner. And keep making that choice and, as events come to mind, choose to forgive and release them to God.

In doing so you will be walking into the fullness of the freedom that God has promised you.

Today's reading:

"And when you stand praying, if you hold anything against anyone, forgive him, so that your Father in heaven may forgive you your sins"
Mark 11:25

"Therefore, the kingdom of heaven is like a king who wanted to settle accounts with his servants. As he began the settlement, a man who owed him ten thousand talents was brought to him. Since he was not able to pay, the master ordered that he and his wife and his children and all that he had be sold to repay the debt.

The servant fell on his knees before him. 'Be patient with me' he begged, 'and I will pay back everything.' The servant's master took pity on him, cancelled the debt and let him go.

But when that servant went out, he found one of his fellow servants who owed him a hundred denarii. He grabbed him and began to choke him. 'Pay back what you owe me!' he demanded. His fellow servant fell to his knees and begged him, 'Be patients with me, and I will pay you back.' But he refused. Instead, he went off and had the man thrown into prison until he could pay the debt. When the other servants saw what had happened, they were greatly distressed and went and told their master everything that had happened.

Then the master called the servant in. 'You wicked servant,' he said, 'I cancelled all that debt of yours because you begged me to. Shouldn't you have had mercy on your fellow servant just as I had on you?' In anger his master turned him over to the jailers to be tortured, until he should pay back all he owed. This is how my heavenly Father will treat each of you unless you forgive your brother from your heart."
Matthew 18:23-35

You can die unsaved, but you cannot die unloved.

There is nothing we can do to make God love us more. There is nothing we can do to make God love us less.

What awesome truth! God loves you just where you are right now. God loves you just as you are right now. God knew from the very beginning all that you would do – and yet He still chose to love you – and chooses to love you still.

Abundant love – Gods love for you is completely over the top. He didn't just meet you half way – He came himself to make a way for you. He gave everything He had – His best – for you. No half measures, no broken promises, He gave His all, for you.

Gods love epitomises the unconditional love that your heart hungers for. God loves you in the way that your heart yearns for. Simply accept and receive His love today.

Choose to see yourself as God sees you today – as the apple of His eye, His beloved daughter, precious in His sight – and allow these truths to permeate deep into your soul.

Today's reading:

"For God so loved the world that he gave is only son that whosoever believes in Him should not perish but have everlasting life."
John 3:16

Some years ago I purchased a book about hearing the voice of God. At the time I felt as if I wasn't hearing from God and maybe I was expecting something more awesome and forceful than the ways in which God does actually speak to us.

Imagine my amazement when I found not just one or two but <u>many</u> different ways in which God speaks to us today and realised that I was already hearing the voice of the Father.

The author described the way we can be sat in church and feel as if the minister is speaking to us personally and must know all that has happened to us during the week. Or the way we might read our Bible and somehow what we are reading relates directly to our experience. Maybe the quiet feeling in our heart when we just know that God has spoken – or even, as some have experienced, an audible voice. Sometimes a friend may say something that confirms a whisper that we have felt in our hearts and minds. Even through our circumstances God can speak to us – sometimes He even uses them to get our attention!

As we step out in faith as we hear God's voice – there is a sense in which it doesn't matter whether we have heard correctly or not. Our Father is so excited at what we will do for Him when we think that we have heard His voice – He is going to make sure that we hear from Him in the future!

Today's reading:

"Today if you hear his voice do not harden your hearts."
Psalm 95: 7-8

"...if anyone hears my voice and opens the door, I will come and eat with him, and he with me."
Revelation 3:20

Who am I? This is a question that it's easy to wrestle with. We can think of ourselves as a daughter, mother, work colleague, wife, sister, helper, friend but not really understand who we truly are.

However you may be feeling today, all of the following are true.

If you have asked forgiveness and committed your life and your ways to Him you can know that you are:

- a child of God (Romans 8:16)

- saved by grace through faith (Ephesians 2:8)

- an heir of eternal life (1 John 5:11-12)

- forgiven (Ephesians 1:7)

- a new creation (2 Corinthians 5:17)

- strong in the Lord and in His mighty power (Ephesians 6:10)

- living by faith and not by sight (2 Corinthians 5:7)

- an heir of God and co-heir with Christ (Romans 8:17)
- blessed with every spiritual blessing (Ephesians 1:3)
- healed by His wounds (1 Peter 2:24)
- being transformed by the renewing of my mind (Romans 12:2)
- doing all things through Christ who gives me strength (Philemon 4:13)
- more than a conqueror (Romans 8:37)

Why not choose to meditate on just one of these promises today?

Sometimes we blame our feeling of being weighed down by the cares of this world on God, especially after we have prayed about it, seemingly without an answer.

The story that follows illustrates that perhaps we need to look at our own response.

"A missionary living in a foreign country once asked his housemaid to fetch the Bible from the bedside table and bring it downstairs. Later that day, he found the Bible still sitting on the bedside table. On talking to the girl he asked why she had not followed his instructions. Her reply was that she had indeed brought the Bible downstairs and then had returned it to its usual place next to the bed."

This cultural misunderstanding so beautifully illustrates what we often do with those things that weigh us down. We take them to the Lord but often walk away again carrying them with us just as before. The Lord wants us to leave them with him and walk away unburdened and free to do all that He has planned for us.

He does this all because "He cares for you" – isn't that an awesome truth? The God who set the stars in their place cares for you, the God who declared "let there be light" cares for you, the God who "makes the clouds his chariot and rides on the wings of the wind" cares for you!

Today, 'take your burdens to the cross and leave them there'.

Today's reading:

"Cast all your anxiety on him because He cares for you."
1 Peter 5:7

In the Old Testament it tells us of a memorable occasion when Joshua led the people across the Jordan river which at that time was in full flood. As the priests carrying the ark of the covenant reached the Jordan and their feet touched the water's edge, the water from upstream stopped flowing... The priests who carried the ark... stood firm on dry ground while all Israel passed by until the whole nation had completed the crossing on dry ground.

To commemorate this amazing miracle Joshua instructed them to take up twelve stones from the middle of the Jordan from right where the priests stood and to carry them over with them and put them down where they stayed that night. When the children asked in the future what the stones meant those who remembered were to tell them the story of how the flow of the Jordan was cut off for the people to cross the Jordan – something to be a memorial for the people.

In our lives we may have occasional mountaintop experiences but also tend to spend quite some time in the valleys in between! We may not have stones today but we have times when we know that God has met with us in some way.

Why not put a mental stake in the mountaintop to help us remember that God did indeed meet with us?

When we are down in the valley we can look back up at the mountain and see the stake reminding us of that special experience of God. For the Israelites it was to be a reminder of what God had done for them and to encourage them that they were His special children. It's the same for us today!

Today's reading:

Joshua 3:14-4:9

I have to confess that it was a huge relief to me to gain a better understanding of today's familiar verse in Isaiah.

I had always felt that the many days when I wasn't 'soaring like an eagle' were somehow less than perfect – probably even a failure as a Christian woman.

God's word tells us that there are spiritual seasons. There will be times when we soar like eagles – but there will also be times of running and simply walking. We also read how important it is sometimes just to stand your ground. There are also times when God Himself is carrying us.

Whether you feel you are soaring, running, walking or barely managing to stand – be encouraged that today your God promises to renew your strength.

Today's reading:

"But those who hope in the Lord will renew their strength. They will soar on wings like eagles; they will run and not grow weary, they will walk and not be faint."
Isaiah 40:31

"Therefore, put on the full armor of God, so that when the day of evil comes, you may be able to stand your ground, and after you have done everything, to stand."
Ephesians 6:13

"be patient and stand firm, because the Lord's coming is near."
James 5:8

Sometimes when we are going through a tough time, we believe that God has indeed abandoned us and that He no longer has a plan and a purpose for our lives.

You may be familiar with the story of Joseph and his colored coat, but we often don't consider the story in much detail as to how it might apply to our lives.

Joseph was falsely accused of adultery with Potiphars wife and was imprisoned for a number of years. It would have been easy for him to feel angry, indignant and wronged. However, the Bible tells us that "while Joseph was there in the prison, the Lord was with him" (Genesis 39:20:21). Joseph allowed God to turn his time in prison to one of precious times with His creator.

While he was in prison, two of the king's officials had offended the king and were imprisoned. It was Joseph's compassion and concern for the king's officials that gave him an opportunity to interpret their dreams. Despite all that had happened to him Joseph still chose to follow God and to point others to Him. One of the officials, the cupbearer, promised to remember him and show him kindness if all went well with him. Yet two years later Joseph was still languishing in prison! When Pharaoh had some strange dreams the cupbearer eventually remembered Joseph and how he had correctly interpreted his dream. Joseph ultimately became Pharaohs right-hand man – but not without a long time of waiting and preparation.

So often when God is taking us through what appears to be a dark valley and we feel abandoned – it is then that He is wanting to build something in us, to root us in Him and to strengthen us. We are often faced with a choice: to focus and depend on ourselves whilst growing bitter and resentful, or to focus and depend on Him and to follow the path where He leads us.

Today's reading:

"Then Pharaoh said to Joseph, "Since God has made all this known to you, there is no one so discerning and wise as you. You shall be in charge of my palace, and all my people are to submit to your orders. Only with respect to the throne will I be greater than you." So Pharaoh said to Joseph, "I hereby put you in charge of the whole land of Egypt." Then Pharaoh took his signet ring from his finger and put it on Joseph's finger. He dressed him in robes of fine linen and put a gold chain around his neck. He had him ride in a chariot as his second-in-command, and men shouted before him, "Make way!". Thus he put him charge of the whole land of Egypt."
Genesis 4:39:41

God call himself your Father, whatever your own experiences of a father, here's how God feels about you.

If God had a photo album, do you know whose photograph would be on the first page? Yours!

If He went to parties, He'd be telling stories of how proud He is of you. You are always on His mind.

The God who created the stars and the seas loves you and is thinking about You right now. You are the apple of His eye.

He loves you. He knows everything (yes, every single thing) about you and He still loves you.

There is nothing that you do that makes Him loves you any less, there is nothing you can do that can make Him love you any more.

Just as in the story of the prodigal son, where the Father is eagerly waiting for the return of His son, so your Father is waiting for you.

He longs to wrap you in his arms and tell you just how much He loves you.

Do you need to run back into the Father's arms today? Spend a few moments now just ask Him to forgive any wrong thoughts or actions and ask Him to wrap His loving arms around you.

Today's reading:

"But while he was still a long way off, his father saw him and was filled with compassion for him; he ran to his son, threw his arms around him and kissed him."
Luke 15:20

Do you know that your salvation does not depend on you?

Your ticket to eternal life isn't <u>dependent</u> on your good works, regular bible study or church attendance.

In this world, so often, we see broken promises. In many marriages today broken promises lead to broken relationships.

The promises of God are not like the promises that we may make elsewhere in life – at work, in marriage, or in our families. These promises (or covenants) usually depend on two people.

You've probably heard someone quote "Let go and let God". The amazing thing about the covenant that we have with God is that only depends on Him to keep it. We may think that we are holding on to Him but the truth really is that it is not dependent upon our strength but upon His. The truth is that it is He that is holding on to us.

He has promised that He will never leave us nor forsake us. We also need to remember that He will never let us go – once His, we are always His.

However weak you feel today, remember that you are not dependent on our frail grasp of his hand, but on His firm hold on yours!

Today's reading:

"You hold me by my right hand."
Psalm 73:23

"This is the covenant I will make with the house of Israel after that time, " declared the Lord. "I will put my laws in their minds and write it on their hearts. I will be their God and they will be my people."
Jeremiah 31:33

Among today's Christians there seems to be a general feeling that becoming a Christian means that we are somehow entitled to God's blessing but none of the trials of this world. It is sometimes hinted or implied in Christian circles that our trials are the outcome of our disobedience. These are modern day "Jobs comforters". Yet, as Job himself said, "Shall we accept good from God, and not trouble?" (Job 1:10) Jesus himself suffered hunger, homelessness and pain – should we genuinely expect our life to be completely free from suffering and pain?

Whilst every one of Gods promises holds true for each believer today – they do not promise a life of ease. Rather God's promises tell us that "When you pass through the waters I will be with you" (Isaiah 43:2), "He will wipe every tear from their eyes" (Rev 21:4), "whoever comes to me I will never drive away" (John 6:37), "God is our refuge and strength, an ever-present help in trouble" (Psalm 46.1), "If you seek Him, he will be found by you" (1 Chronicles 28:9).

Paul, author of several of the books in the New Testament, also suffered many trials. Trials are just a part of our Christian walk and God often used them to draw us closer to Him.

The good news is that whatever happens, we are no longer alone. We have a God who will walk through the darkest of valleys with us and give us strength when we need it.

Today's reading:

"Are they Hebrews? So am I. Are they Israelites? So am I. Are they Abraham's descendants? So am I. I am more. I have worked much harder, been in prison more frequently, been flogged more severely, and been exposed to death again and again. Five times I received from the Jews the forty lashes minus one. Three times I was beaten with rods, once I was stoned, three times I was shipwrecked, I spent a night and a day in the open sea, I have been constantly on the move. I have been in danger from rivers, in danger from bandits, in danger from my own countrymen, in danger from Gentiles; in danger in the city, in danger in the country, in danger at sea; and in danger from false brothers... I have known hunger and thirst and have often gone without food; I have been cold and naked."

2 Corinthians 11: 22-27

Today I would like to share with you something that I wrote a while ago:-

"You won't find what you're looking for in the places you once walked or the answer to your questions in the faces of the past.

Let go, put down, yes, leave behind the tangle of what's been, remember but the beauty in all that you have seen.

This pain of letting go is a part of moving on to all that God has planned for you and the blessings that will come.

One single solitary constant in this unholy mess, the Tower, Gods love, unmoved, now with us all our life.

That ever present love is what will see us through, though people fail and falter there's One that never moves.

Hold on to Him and seek His face, His loving arms will help you to complete life's race."

Looking back to the past can be painful and drag us down. It can hinder us from moving forward into the fullness of God's plan for us.

When the time comes to let go, don't be afraid to say "yes" to God and move forward, with Him into the future He has planned for you.

Today's reading:

"For as high as the heavens are above the earth, so great is his love for those who fear him; as far as the east is from the west, so far has he removed our transgressions from us."
Psalm 103:11-12

May I ask you two questions? Who do you believe you are? Whose view of yourself do you accept?

If we accept what we have heard about ourselves from the words and actions of those around us we may see our failures and not our true potential.

One of the best gifts you could receive today would be that you would start to see yourself as God sees you. If you start to believe even a minute fraction of what He sees inside you then it has the potential to radically change your life.

Sociologists suggest that we become what the most important person in our life thinks that we are. If they are right and if we choose to make God number one in our life and believe His words about us – we can become the world changers we are called to be. More than that though – we can become truly at peace with who and what we are.

If you can catch a glimpse of the love that God has for you, begin to understand the plans and purposes He has for you, it's the beginning of a life changing relationship.

Today's reading:

"For I have loved you with an everlasting love..."

Have you ever heard ~~the~~ the voice of God? There are many people who earnestly desire to hear from God and yet feel that there is a wall of silence.

One of the biggest things standing between us and God is unforgiveness in our hearts. When we allow ourselves to become angry or bitter we build up a wall between us and God which only comes tumbling down when we acknowledge it and ask His forgiveness.

Hearing Him also involves our faith. We need to trust that God is wanting to speak to us and starting to allow ourselves to listen.

If we create opportunities for Him to speak – then we will surely get better at hearing His voice. Reading the Bible regularly and attending a church where we can hear the word of God preached can certainly help. How about having a time of the day where you stop long enough to listen – to allow yourself a time of peace and quiet – and just to listen.

And last, but by no means least, ASK! God loves to give us good things. If we ask Him to help us learn to hear His voice we are asking for something that He is also longing for. His answer is an unequivocal YES!!

Today's reading:

"Ask and it will be given to you; seek and you will find; knock and the door will be opened to you."
Matthew 7:7

"He makes me lie down in green pastures, he leads me beside quiet waters, he restores my soul."
Psalm 23:2-3

The Bible tells us that God's ways and our ways are often very different.

When God wants to build something in our lives He often sweeps away all the current structures, roles and works that we have become familiar with. Although we may see them as useful and comforting, sometimes even the good things need to be removed from our lives, in order for God to build something even greater.

Jesus describes this in a story about the vinedresser. "...every branch that does bear fruit he prunes so that it will be even more fruitful."

When you see the luxuriant growth on the grape vine and the heavily laden branches – it seems almost illogical to believe that cutting this growth back to the hard stumpy root is the way to even more fruit the following year. Yet each year, the vineyard is harshly trimmed in order to become more fruitful the following year. This can be as true in our lives as it is in nature, when God comes bringing change and new growth.

God does not always even cut out those things which are not good – sometimes what He removes is good because He has something even better planned for us. Continue to place your trust in Him as you see Him at work in your life.

Today's reading:

"For my thoughts are not your thoughts, neither are your ways my says," declares the Lord. *"As the heavens are higher than the earth, so are my ways higher than your ways and my thoughts than your thoughts."*
Isaiah 55:8-9

Are you feeling overwhelmed? Thinking about giving up or quitting?

When we are battling or struggling in our own strength, it's easy to think that we can't manage, that we're simply not strong enough.

At times like this it's so important to remember the good news, which is that you and God are a majority.

Whatever opposition you are struggling against today, remember this simple maths:-

Me + God = A MAJORITY

Are you the sort of person who is about read a book and is always tempted to look at the final few pages to see how it ends? Well, the best news is that the final chapter of the Bible says that we WIN!!

Jesus promises "*I am coming soon*" (Revelation 22:20) and "*...if I go and prepare a place for you, I will come back and take you to be with me...*" (John 14:3)

Today's reading:

"If God is for us, who can be against us?"
Romans 8:31

This well-known Psalm needs no introduction – many of us are familiar with these comforting words.

These simple words provide an assurance that God already knows that we are going to walk through dark places ("the shadow of death") and that He is already walking ahead of us.

He promises to restore our soul and provide all that we need.

Today, re-read this familiar Psalm in your own Bible and choose to rest in these promises of God.

Today's reading:

"The Lord is my shepherd, I shall not be in want. He makes me lie down in green pastures, he leads me beside quiet waters, he restores my soul. He guides me in the paths of righteousness for his name's sake. Even though I walk through the valley of the shadow of death, I will fear no evil, for you are with me; your rod and your staff, they comfort me.

You prepare a table before me in the presence of my enemies. You anoint my head with oil; my cup overflows. Surely goodness and love will follow me all the days of my life, and I will dwell in the house of the Lord forever."

Psalm 23

Some years ago I was present in a service where the preacher confidently declared that, of course, there were no such thing as modern day lepers. My heart leapt and I wanted to stand up in that church and tell him that he was wrong – even in our modern churches sadly there are still lepers – people who are excluded simply because they are in some way different. As a divorced woman I knew that too well – and I am sure there are other individuals who have found just the same.

Yet the good news is that God wants to use you, even in your brokenness, maybe even through all that is and has happened to you.

Artie Gardella, a minister in New York, once said "God cannot use a man or woman greatly until they have been broken deeply".

This is so true – those of us who have experienced brokenness know how to help and minister to others who are going through difficult times.

Those of us who have experienced this brokenness have so much to offer the hurting church. When the time is right, we need to rise up and show Gods love and care to those around us. We need to show Gods acceptance of each individual whatever their circumstances – for we know His heart towards the lost and hurting.

Today's reading:

"My grace is sufficient for you, for my power is made perfect in weakness."
2 Corinthians 12:9

"Praise be to the God and Father of our Lord Jesus Christ, the Father of compassion and the God of all comfort, who comforts us in all our troubles, so that we can comfort those in any trouble with the comfort we ourselves have received from God."
2 Corinthians 1:3-4

One of the common reasons for people stopping or not wanting to come to church, is that they have been disappointed with how so-called Christians have behaved towards them or to others.

It is very easy to confuse God with his representatives here on earth – the church and the Christians that make up that church. We have all heard stories or have our own experiences of how insensitive and hurtful both the church and Christians can be.

It's very to make a clear and important distinction. Although God is in His church and works through it – the church is NOT God.

Similarly, although God resides in Christians, they are still only sinners saved by grace and as such are all 'working towards' perfection.

It reminds me of the saying you may have heard, "If you find a perfect church, don't join it, you'll only spoil it." It's so true, that we smile, but forget that each church is made up of broken people, just like us.

Even if you've been hurt by Christians, had them disappoint you or let you down, don't use this as a way to shut God out – but rather consider that He is the only one that you can trust and always rely on.

Today's reading:

"If any one of you is without sin, let him be the first to throw a stone at her... Woman, where are they? Has no one condemned you?"
John 8:7

What are you afraid of today? What fears are ruling and shaping your life?

For a number of years a single postcard has remained at the centre of my kitchen noticeboard – it reads as follows:

> "NO FEAR
>
> (of anything)
>
> who would dare tangle with God
>
> by messing with one of God's chosen...?"

It is human nature to fear what others may think of you, to fear failure, to fear rejection.

This verse reminds me that if God is for us, who can be against us?

If we are following Him and seeking to follow His plan in our lives – then we have all of heaven backing us up – whom shall we fear?

Today's reading:

"who would dare tangle with God by messing with one of God's chosen...?"
Romans 8:33 (The Message)

It was a normal day. I'd just dropped my daughter at work and decided to pop in and fill up the tank in my car. As I went to pay I was surprised by the attitude of the elderly gentleman attendant. He took the time to wish me a relaxing weekend and hoped there would not be too much washing to do (I had just bought washing powder in addition to my fuel). He then wished me a very pleasant New Year and smiled at me as I left the shop.

How refreshing it was to see and experience grace in action! Grace can be an unexpected kindness when we least expect or deserve it. A small effort on behalf of the giver made a big difference to my attitude through the rest of my day.

How many times did the writers of New Testament letters wish their readers "grace" – "Grace and peace to you", "Grace be with you".

Each act of grace is like a spray of perfume in a room – a little goes a long way and improves our surroundings.

Ask God for opportunities to minister His grace to those around you – and allow His perfume to fill the air.

Today's reading:

"...make the most of every opportunity. Let your conversation be always full of grace, seasoned with salt, so that you may know how to answer everyone."
Colossians 4:6

"For we are to God the aroma of Christ among those who are being saved and those who are perishing... the fragrance of life."
2 Corinthians 2:15-16

Do past failures make you think that God will never be able to use you?

Think that what you've done is beyond God's grace?

Take a look at three sinners whose names you might know:

David – a young shepherd boy who rose to be King. Major mistakes in life – murder and adultery. Major achievements in life – to be called 'a man after Gods own heart'.

Paul – persecutor of Christians turned evangelist. Major mistakes in life – too religious – stood by whilst Stephen was stoned to death – actively persecuted Christians. Major achievements in life – took the gospel to many countries and wrote several of the books of the Bible.

Moses – Jewish boy turned Egyptian prince. Major mistakes in life – murder. Major achievements in life – leading a whole bunch of lost people into the land that God had promised – talking with God on a mountain.

Still convinced that your sin is unforgiveable?

Come to Jesus and confess it today. Receive Gods forgiveness and move on to all that He has planned for you.

Today's reading:

"Here is a trustworthy saying that deserves full acceptance: Christ Jesus came into this world to save sinners – of whom I am the worst."
1 Timothy 1:15 (Written by Paul)

When the pressures of the world are pressing in upon us – it can be hard to find the strength to carry on. We can allow our feelings to weigh us down and can struggle to feel joy of any kind.

It is not unusual for Christians have these experiences. Despite the smiles you see on faces in church on Sunday, many people go through struggles and difficult times.

We need to know where to turn when we have these feelings – and to have confidence that we will receive what we ask for. The reading in Chronicles tell us that strength and joy are to be found in His dwelling place – but this is not referring to a church building.

Through faith, Christ dwells in our hearts (Ephesians 3:17). As we come together with other believers we "are being built together to become a dwelling in which God lives by his Spirit" (Ephesians 2:22). The words of Chronicles assure us that there will be 'strength and joy in his dwelling place' – that means each of us!

We can come to the throne of grace with complete confidence that we will receive strength and be filled with joy. It's God promise to us and He is always faithful.

Today's reading:

"Sing to the Lord, all the earth; proclaim his salvation day after day. Declare his glory among the nations, his marvellous deeds among all peoples. For great is the Lord and most worthy of praise; he is to be feared above all gods. For all the gods of the nations are idols, but the Lord made the heavens. Splendor and majesty are before him; strength and joy in his dwelling place."
1 Chronicles 16:23-27

Sometimes the smallest thing that we do has a bigger impact than we can imagine. Recently a good friend reminded me of a quote I had written out for her many years before. Unbeknown to me she had kept it safely in her jewelry box all that time. She said she had taken it out occasionally to read, something which I had never known until today, when she read it out to me. The quote reads:

"His desire is not to make you happy, His desire is to make you His."

Sometimes it is easy in our Western world to get caught up in the idea that handing over our lives to God means an easy ride.

There's a story about the eagle who, when the young are ready to leave the nest, pushes it out – out of the comfort and security and into all the dangers and risk that the outside world holds. The young eagle learns to fly because it has to, it has no real choice. It could seem like a harsh choice for its parents to make – but the result, a bird of prey soaring in the sky, is one of the most majestic and impressive sights and is the result of it's parents decision to kick it out of it's comfortable nest.

In our lives it seems that God sometimes pushes us out of the nest, our comfort zones, confident that we can rise to the challenge. Sometimes we are not so sure! Whether we are having a day where we soar on wings like eagles, a day where we can run or one where we can barely walk, He will strengthen us if we trust in Him.

Today's reading:

"Those who hope in the Lord will renew their strength. They will soar on wings like eagles, they will run and not grow weary, they will walk and not be faint."
Isaiah 40:31

A missionary returning from years in the mission field was bitterly disappointed with the welcome he received when he returned home. Talking to God he poured out his heart – how his commitment and hard work was worth a better welcome home than he had received.

Gods response was a simple one – "*You're not home yet, son.*"

You're not home yet! As you continue to be faithful in loving & serving Him, you can be assured that the welcome that you will receive in our Fathers kingdom will be awesome and well worth waiting for.

You will be welcomed into a kingdom where we will discover and know all the beauty, intimacy and adventure your heart longs for.

The welcome you receive there will be part of the biggest party and celebration the Kingdom has ever seen.

So today remember, God sees each small way that you serve when no-one sees, and think about the awesome celebration that's gonna take place when you finally arrive in your true "home".

Today's reading:

"...you will receive a rich welcome into the eternal kingdom of our Lord and Saviour Jesus Christ."
2 Peter 1:11

"Well done, good and faithful servant! You have been faithful with a few things; I will put you in charge of many things. Come and share your master's happiness!"
Matthew 25:21

A Final Word or Two

Thanks for taking the time to read through these readings.

I trust that you have found refreshment and encouragement in some small way.

Take encouragement from the small glimmers of light and hope that shine into your world – if we can find a place of thankfulness for these small mercies, then God can work miracles in and around us!

And finally a reminder – life will not always feel like it does today.

It may feel as if you have been in a dark place for ever, but our God is a God who delights in rescuing His people. He has an eternal destiny for you and you have His sure promise that you will spend eternity together with Him.

About the Author

Jennifer has been writing and publishing since 2004.

She has written a number of Christian titles which have been published as ebooks, including "Free Christian Stuff for Churches". She is passionate about building the local church.

Jennifer has three grown up children and one granddaughter. She lives in Wiltshire, close to the cathedral city of Salisbury.

You can find her latest books & devotionals at
www.hopebooks.org

Order Details

All our titles may be ordered via Amazon

Some of our titles are also available on Kindle. Kindle is available to download to your PC, Mac, iPhone or Android phone.

For any difficulties obtaining a copy of any title, please send an email to:
orders@hopebooks.org

Printed in Great Britain
by Amazon